FLOR PEETERS

LITTLE ORGAN BOOK

For

Beginners in Organ Playing

Includes Graded Exercises on Well-Known Hymn Tunes

Summy-Birchard Inc.
Exclusively distributed by
Alfred Publishing co., Inc.

ISBN 087487-600-1

INDEX OF CONTENTS

Flor Peeters' Practice Organ.. IV

I Foreword

    The Instrument.. V

      Wind Mechanism

      Action

      Pipework

    Elementary Rules for Organ Playing................................... X

      Position at the Organ

      How to Practice

    Registration.. XI

      For Choir Accompaniment

      For Organ Literature

    Index of Hymn Tunes and Original Compositions..................... XII

II Elementary Exercises: Attack, Legato,............................... 1

    Crossing, Substitution, Glissando,

    Rules for Performance

III Two-part Manual Playing... 8

IV Elementary Pedal Exercises (toes):................................ 18

    Attack, Intervals, Studies

V Three-part Playing... 25

    Preparatory Two-part Exercise for one Hand

    Three-part Manual Playing.. 28

VI Pedal Exercises for Toe and Heel................................. 43

VII Two-part Manual and Pedal Playing............................. 50

VIII Three-part Manual and Pedal Playing.......................... 56

IX Four-part Manual Playing.. 82

X Four-part Manual and Pedal Playing............................. 88

Flor Peeters' Smallest Practice Organ

Pipe Specifications for Practice Organ:
　　Rohrflöte 8'
　　Prestant 4'
　　Rohrflöte 4'
　　Octave 2'
　　Cimbel 3r
Extra rank for Pedal:
　　Resultantbas 16'

Instrument has five ranks of pipes available on each manual and in the pedal, with an extra rank in the pedal

I. FOREWORD

THE INSTRUMENT

The organ is a many-voiced wind instrument. The wind pressure is supplied by a blower and bellows. The musical sound is produced directly by the organist who manipulates the keys and the stops at the console.

The console of a complete organ has two manuals and a pedal keyboard. Organ consoles for large organs often have three or four manuals and a pedal keyboard. Organs are usually designed for specific purposes and locations. If an organ for example, is to be used primarily for choir accompaniments in a particular church of given dimensions, it will be designed tonally for that purpose and given a physical shape for that place. If, on the other hand, it is to be used as a solo and ensemble instrument in a concert hall, the tonal and physical design will be different.

The principal parts of the organ are:

1) The **wind mechanism** (heavy pressure bellows, trunking, regulating bellows, etc.)

2) The **action,** (windchest, soundboard, pallets, manuals, etc.)

3) The **pipework** (sound-producing part of the organ)

Wind mechanism

What the lungs are for a singer, the bellows are for the organ, supplying as they do the compressed wind and holding it in readiness for use. The windtrunk or channel conducts the wind from the heavy-pressure bellows to the windchest and soundboard. An important element is the regulating bellows which serves to keep the wind at a steady pressure.

Action

The action includes the soundboard, the slides, pallets and stop mechanism. There are three types of action; **mechanical,** operated by means of a lever; **pneumatic,** by **windpressure;** and **electric,** by means of electric magnets. The soundboard or chest is the heart of the organ where the mechanism of the action and that of the stops cooperate in producing sound from the pipes.

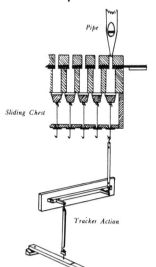

Pipe

Sliding Chest

Tracker Action

The **keyboards** and **pedals** consist of a certain number of keys the manipulation of which controls the action. Each stop has its own distinctive tone-color and pitch, while each keyboard has its own tone character owing to the distinctive family of stops it governs. The keyboards or manuals are placed in terrace formation. They can be coupled together and to the pedals. Thus we have manual and pedal couplers as well as octave and sub-octave couplers which raise or lower the pitch by an octave.

The usual keyboard arrangements are the following:

1) Organ with two manuals:

> Swell or Choir — Upper keyboard
> Great — Lower keyboard

2) Organ with three manuals:

> Swell — Topmost keyboard
> Great — Middle keyboard
> Choir — Lowest keyboard

3) Organ with four manuals:

> Solo — Topmost keyboard
> Swell — Upper middle keyboard
> Great — Lower middle keyboard
> Choir — Lowest keyboard

Pipework

The pipes as the sources of musical sound, constitute the most important component of the organ. Pipes differ in form, dimension and material. The form may be cylindrical, conical or pyramidal. Material may be wood or metal of various kinds. Pipes are called **flues** (labials) or **reeds** (linguals) according to their distinctive tone quality or timbre. The pitch in flue-pipes is determined by the length, width and form of the pipe; in the reeds by the tongue and the boot.

A **register** (stop) is a series of organ pipes from the largest to the smallest, homogeneous in timbre and intensity, each pipe corresponding to a key on the manual. A drawstop or stop-key on the console brings the series into play. These registers or pipe series are divided into seven families, according to timbre. These families are: **Diapason, Flute, Bourdon, String, Mutation, Mixture,** and **Reed.** A pipe corresponds to each key, except in the case of the mixture where there is more than one pipe to each key.

The relative pitch of registers is expressed in terms of feet. The pitch of the eight-foot register (8') is that of the piano. Generally speaking, the pipe of the lowest C of an eight-foot register is eight feet long. A register half that length (4') will sound an octave higher, and a register double that length (16') will sound an octave lower, and so on, according to the ordinary laws of acoustics.

A **mutation stop** is a register which does not produce the normal note of the key played, but a natural harmonic of that note. The nazard 2 2/3 (quint) produces the third natural harmonic or 12th.

The **mixtures** add combinations of super harmonics, varying in number according to the number of ranks engaged, the number being frequently indicated on the stop. Mixture 4r = four harmonics. Above a certain point on the keyboard, special modifications have to be employed by the builder as the harmonics would be of too high a pitch to be practicable or audible. These modifications are termed "breaks" or "returns".

Combination of a 4 to 5r mixture with indication of the breaks:

C	$1\frac{1}{3}$	1	$\frac{2}{3}$	$\frac{1}{2}$	
g^0	2	$1\frac{1}{3}$	1	$\frac{2}{3}$	$\frac{1}{2}$
c^1	$2\frac{2}{3}$	2	$1\frac{1}{3}$	1	$\frac{2}{3}$
g^1	4	$2\frac{2}{3}$	2	$1\frac{1}{3}$	1
g^2	4	4	$2\frac{2}{3}$	2	$1\frac{1}{3}$

Combination of a 3r Cimbel with indication of the breaks:

C	$\frac{1}{4}$	$\frac{1}{6}$	$\frac{1}{8}$
c^0	$\frac{1}{3}$	$\frac{1}{4}$	$\frac{1}{6}$
f^0	$\frac{1}{2}$	$\frac{1}{3}$	$\frac{1}{4}$
c^1	$\frac{2}{3}$	$\frac{1}{2}$	$\frac{1}{3}$
f^1	1	$\frac{2}{3}$	$\frac{1}{2}$
c^2	$1\frac{1}{3}$	1	$\frac{2}{3}$
f^2	2	$1\frac{1}{3}$	1
c^3	$2\frac{2}{3}$	2	$1\frac{1}{3}$

Combinations.

There are two kinds of combinations: the "fixed" combination and the "free" combination.

The "fixed" combination is placed beneath the manuals in the form of a thumb-piston and when pressed brings on groups of stops. The thumb-pistons bear the labels: PP (pianissimo), P (piano), F (forte), FF (fortissimo) and T (tutti). These "fixed" combination pistons are falling into disuse in most modern organ building. They are called "fixed" because the organist may not change at will the stops governed by each of the pistons.

The "free" combinations on the other hand, are of greater benefit and importance. Like the fixed combination, these are usually found as thumb-pistons beneath the manuals, but unlike the fixed combination piston, the stops which each "free" piston brings on can be prepared at will by the organist. In this way he can prepare as many combinations of stops as there are pistons on the organ. In the case of a large instrument, these adjustable or "free" combinations can be of inestimable value in placing at the disposal of the organist the many tonal colors contained in the instrument. The "free" combination pistons are arranged in numerical sequence for pedal and each of the manuals.
There are often combination pistons known as "general" pistons which control the entire tonal resources of the organ.

The **Swell Pedal.** A section of the instrument is enclosed behind a series of shutters which are capable of being gradually opened and closed by means of a foot level "swell pedal" By the use of this pedal, a controlled crescendo or diminuendo is made possible and greater expressiveness attained.

The **General Crescendo** pedal. (Roll-Schweller), gradually brings into play all the stops of the organ from the softest up to the full power of the instrument.

Finally, here follows a list of the names of the stops in general use, classified in families:

DIAPASONS:
Prestant 16', 8' or 4'
Diapason 16', 8' or 4'
Principal 16', 8' or 4'
Montre 8'
Contrebasse 16'
Octave 8', 4' or 2'
Doublette 2'

FLUTES:
Block flute 8', 4' or 2'
Clarabella 8'
Concert Flute 8'
Flute Traversiere 4'
Flageolet 2', 1'
Open Flute, Wood Flute 8'
Flute dolce 8'
Rohrflöte 8', 4'
Spitzflöte 8', 4' or 2'
Waldflöte 2'
Flute harmonique 8', 4'

STRINGS:
Gamba 8'
Violinbass 16'
Dolce 8'
Salicional 8'
Fugara 8', 4'
Spitzgamba 8'
Eoline 8'
Gemshorn 8', 4'
Viola 8'
Viola di gamba 8'
Cello 8'
Voix celeste 8'

BOURDONS:
(Gedeckt) Gedeckt 32', 16', 8', 4'
Bourdon 16', 8'
Sub-bass 32', 16'
Nachthorn 16', 8', 4', 2'
Quintenbass 16', 8'
Hohlflöte or Hohlpfeife 8', (4')

MUTATIONS:
Quint 10 2/3, 5 1/3, 2 2/3, 1 1/3
Grossnasat 5 1/3
Nazard 2 2/3
Grossterz 6 2/3
Tierce 3 1/5, 1 3/5
Septième (seventh) 4 4/7, 2 2/7, 1 1/7

MIXTURES:
Mixture 3, 4, 5, 6, 7 to 8 ranks and more
Plein Jeu 3, 4 or 5 R
Cimbal 3 to 7 R
Cornet 3 to 5 and 6 R
Progressio 3 to 5 R
Sharp mixture 3 to 5 R
Carillon 2 to 3 R
Rauschpfeife 3 to 7 R
Sesquialter 2 (to 3) R
Tertian 2 R

REEDS:
Trumpet 16', 8', 4'
Bombarde 32', 16'
Posaune 32', 16'
Clarion 4'
Zink 2'
Tuba 16', 8'
Dulcian 8'
Dulcian Regal 16'
Fagotte 16'
Bassoon 16'
Oboe 8' (4')
Horn 8'
Chalumeau 8', 4'
Cromorne 8'
Bärpfeife 8', 4'
Ranket 16'
Sordun 32', 16'
Clarionet 8'
Cor anglais 8'
Vox humana 8'
Regal 8', 4'

The following chart is a scheme of fundamentals and mutation stops indicating the pitch they produce:

Stop in feet	Pitch in relation to note played	Harmonic Series					
		32'	16'	8'	4'	2'	1'
32'	two octaves lower	1st					
16'	one octave lower	2nd	1st				
10⅔'	a perfect fourth lower	3rd					
8'	normal pitch of note played	4th	2nd	1st			
6-2/5'	a major third higher	5th					
5⅓'	a perfect fifth higher	6th	3rd				
4-4/7'	a minor seventh lower	7th					
4'	one octave higher		4th	2nd	1st		
3-1/5'	one octave and a third higher		5th				
2⅔'	one octave and a fifth higher		6th	3rd			
2-2/7'	one octave and a seventh higher		7th				
2'	two octaves higher			4th	2nd	1st	
1-3/5'	two octaves and a third higher			5th			
1⅓'	two octaves and a fifth higher			6th	3rd		
1-1/7'	two octaves and a seventh higher			7th			
1'	three octaves higher				4th	2nd	1st

ELEMENTARY RULES FOR ORGAN PLAYING

Position at the Organ

Correct bodily position is of great importance because of its effect on the technique of performance.

The organist seated in the middle of the seat, must hold his body erect sufficiently inclined forward to se-

Flor Peeters

showing

correct

position

at Console

of an Organ

cure comfortable reach of the manuals. His posture remains quiet while playing with the elbows close to the

body and hands flexible and firm when in contact with the keys. The attack must be decisive with flexible elastic fingers. During solo pedal passages the hands may rest on the seat. The position of the feet is of equal importance. Generally speaking the knees and feet should be held close together, the feet maintaining contact with the pedals. During a prolonged rest, the right foot may be placed on the swell pedal. Attack and release must be quick and decisive.

How to Practice

Much time and effort are wasted by unprepared, unmethodical practice. Many players know a piece only after playing it over and over again. It is a mechanical manner of playing without intelligent grasp of the composition.

Analytic study must prevail. No matter how simple a composition, its structure should be analyzed before actual practice at the keyboard.

In the beginning, all playing should be **very slow,** each hand and the pedals separately. In polyphonic works the student must decide by previous study to which hand each section of an inner part is to be assigned.

Where finger and pedal marks are not supplied, the student should determine these only after careful study and actual trial. Once determined this fingering and pedalling should be memorized and permanently retained.

After practicing each hand and pedals separately, both hands may be practiced together; then each hand separately with the pedals; and finally, manuals and pedals combined.

REGISTRATION

For Choir Accompaniment

For Plain Chant registration, preference should be given to 8' stops of neutral tone-color, e.g., Bourdon 8', Gemshorn 8', Cor-de-Nuit 8', Clarabella 8', Flute a Cheminée 8', Soft Flute 8' (not the Harmonic Flute 8') or a soft old-style Principal 8'; with a Bourdon 16' in the pedals, all this nicely adapted to the strength of the choir that is to be accompanied. For the accompaniment of children's or women's choir, a soft 4' stop may be added, which is also advisable for a small mixed choir.

For a large body of singers (congregation) or for a large mixed choir, the organist may add according to the strength of the voices, the position of the organ, the size of the building, strong 8' and 4' stops, as well as 2', even mixtures on the Great, and sometimes also a soft 16' stops. Stops of a pronounced string quality should not be employed in the accompaniment; they sustain less successfully, attract too much attention, and lack the dignity and reverence proper to this essentially sacred music. A soft 16' pedal with a discreet 8' added best sustains the voices, and thus maintains pitch. Perhaps it is preferable in the case of the more elaborate melismatic melodies not to use the pedal, or at least to do so with great discretion. If chanters alternate with the choir it is well to use the pedal only at each entry of the choir.

For popular hymns and chorales the general rules for proportion are the same as those given for plain chant. It is advisable to accompany chorales sung by a large group with a principal chorus of 8' and 4' and a mixture on the same keyboard. In case one wishes to play the melody in solo, use the foundation 8', 4', 2', plus a Cornet on the first manual or the solo, and 8' and 4' for the accompaniment of the second manual. The pedal should be registered with 16' and 8' stops, and also coupled to the second manual.

For Organ Literature

For organ works of the old and classic literature with a **cantus firmus** melody, use a Cornet 5 ranks, trumpet 8', or softer reeds such as Cromorne 8', Schalmey 8', and Regal 8', either alone or with the addition to the soft reeds of a few mutation stops or a mixture.

Organo Pleno in the classic pre-Bach and Bach periods means generally Principals (Diapasons) 16', 8', 4' and 2', plus mixtures, cymbals and a few not-too-heavy reeds.

A combination of a string (not too small scale) a Salicional 8' and a Nazard 2 2/3' can be used with good results instead of a soft reed, as an Oboe. A Flute 8' (or Bourdon 8') with the same Nazard 2 2/3' is a good imitation of a Clarinet 8' or of a Cromorne 8'. When one mixes a modern Vox Humana 8' with a Rohrflote 4', a Nazard 2 2/3', or a Tierce 1 3/5' (or with the addition of both the latter) the sound is like that of a soft reed, with a color useful in the registration of old organ literature.

For the Old Masters and the classic literature, the organist should not use too many heavy reeds, as they make the polyphonic writing and the voice leading unclear. In Romantic and modern literature the Vox

Celeste 8' is used without tremolo and for harmonic passages only, never for melodic lines or solo. This stop should not be mixed with large flutes or mutation stops.

The registration must be adapted to the tempo of the music and to the place in which one is playing. In a large church the registration should be smaller and clearer than in a concert hall where there is generally not so much reverberation.

The final guide to the art of registration should be what one learns through a good education in artistic taste, the study of organ specifications and organ literature of all styles, and the experience of playing different organs.

Index of Hymn Tunes and Original Compositions

Where hymn tunes are arranged in the form of chorales or chorale-preludes, the voice line which carries the tune is indicated as C. F. (Cantus Firmus).

No.	Title	Composer – Arranger	Form	Page
III.	TWO - PART MANUAL PLAYING			
1	Now, My Tongue, the Myst'ry Telling	Flor Peeters	C. F. in Sop.	8
2	God, My Father, Loving Me	Flor Peeters	C. F. in Bass	9
3	Father, We Thank Thee for the Night	Flor Peeters	C. F. in Sop.	9
4	O Sacred Head	Flor Peeters	C. F. in Tenor	10
5	O Sacred Head	J. Pachelbel	C. F. in Sop.	11
6	Invention	Flor Peeters	—	12
7	Warum sollt ich mich denn grämen	J. G. Walther	Ornamented Melody in Sop.	13
8	Versus VI Toni	A. V. den Kerckhoven	—	14
9	Invention	Flor Peeters	—	15
10	O Gott, du frommer Gott	J. S. Bach	Partita	16
V.	THREE - PART MANUAL PLAYING			
1	Prelude	Flor Peeters	—	28
2	Now My Tongue	Flor Peeters	C. F. in Sop.	29
3	Allein Gott in der Höh sei Ehr	F. W. Zachow	C. F. in Sop.	30
4	Magnificat IV Toni	G. Carissimi	Verset	31
5	Wie schön leuchtet der Morgenstern	D. Buxtehude	C. F. in Sop.	32
6	O Sacred Head	J. Pachelbel	C. F. in Bass	34
7	O Sacred Head	Flor Peeters	C. F. in Sop.	36
8	Veni Creator	Flor Peeters	Invention	38
9	Gottes Sohn ist kommen	J. S. Bach	Fughetta	40
10	O Come, All Ye Faithful	Flor Peeters	C. F. in Sop.	42

No.	Title	Composer – Arranger	Form	Page
VII. TWO - PART MANUAL AND PEDAL PLAYING				
1	Prelude	Flor Peeters	C. F. in Pedal	50
2	Prelude	Flor Peeters	C. F. in Sop.	50
3	Invention	Flor Peeters	—	50
4	God, My Father	Flor Peeters	C. F. in Pedal	51
5	Father, We Thank Thee	Flor Peeters	C. F. in Sop.	51
6	O Sacred Head	Flor Peeters	C. F. in Pedal	52
7	Interlude	J. Habert	—	53
8	Prelude	J. Habert	—	54
VIII. THREE - PART MANUAL AND PEDAL PLAYING				
1	Jesus Christ Is Risen Today	Flor Peeters	C. F. in Sop.	56
2	Creator alme siderum	J. Titelouse	C. F. in Sop.	59
3	O Sacred Head	Flor Peeters	C. F. in Sop.	62
4	Jesus Christ Is Risen Today	Flor Peeters	C. F. in Tenor	64
5	God, Father, Praise and Glory	Flor Peeters	C. F. in Tenor	67
6	Von Himmel hoch	F. W. Zachow	C. F. in Pedal	70
7	Jesus Christ Is Risen Today	Flor Peeters	C. F. in Pedal	72
8	Andante	J. L. Krebs	Three-part	75
9	Von Himmel hoch	J. Pachelbel	C. F. in Pedal	77
10	Unto Thee I Cry, O Lord Jesus	J. S. Bach	Ornamented Melody in Sop.	80
IX. FOUR - PART MANUAL PLAYING				
1	Holy God, We Praise Thy Name	Flor Peeters	Chorale	82
2	Versus VI Toni	A. de Cabezon	—	83
3	Versus I Toni	J. K. Kerll	—	84
4	Liebster Jesu, Wir sind hier	J. S. Bach	Chorale	85
5	Versus V Toni	J. Pachelbel	—	86
X. FOUR - PART MANUAL AND PEDAL PLAYING				
1	Now, My Tongue	Flor Peeters	Chorale	88
2	Dernier Kyrie (From Gregorian Mass No. IV)	F. Couperin	C. F. in Pedal	90
3	Herr Gott, lass dich erbarmen	H. Isaac	Chorale	92
4	Jesu meine Freude	J. S. Bach	Ornamented Mel.	94
5	Gelobet seist du, Jesu Christ	J. S. Bach	C. F. in Sop.	96
6	Prelude and Fugue in C	J. S. Bach	—	100

II. Elementary Exercises

Attack

Keep the hands motionless and the fingers in contact with the keys throughout the exercise.   Practice hands separately at first.

1

2

3

M. & R. Co. 5091

2

Legato

Perfect legato playing is an elementary and essential factor in organ playing.   There must be no break in the line as fingers pass from one note to another; nor must there be an overlapping of the tones.

Legato and staccato notes

M. & R. Co. 5091

Crossing of the thumb

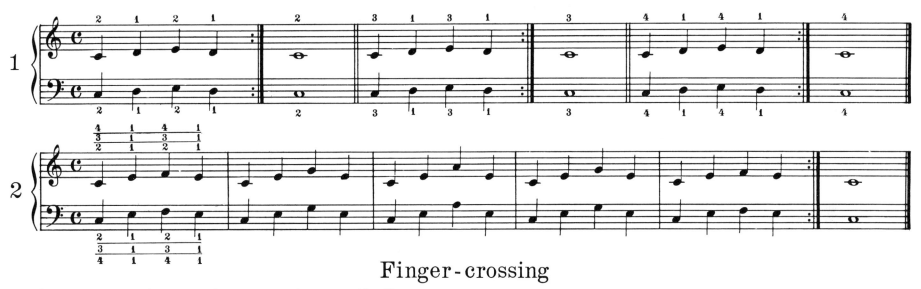

Finger-crossing

A line over the figure indicates crossing *over* the finger.
A line under the figure indicates crossing *under* the finger.

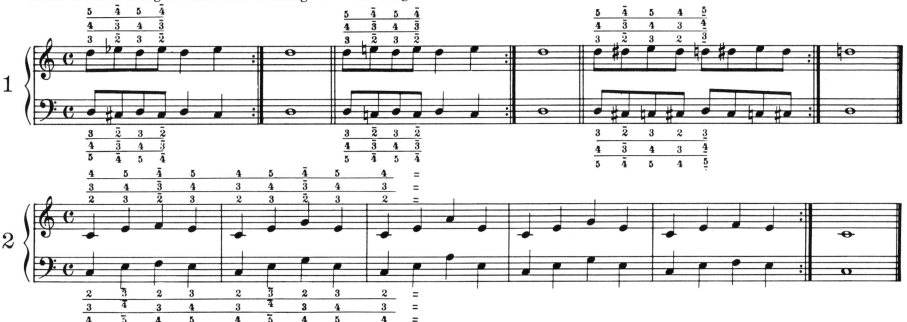

M. & R. Co. 5091

4

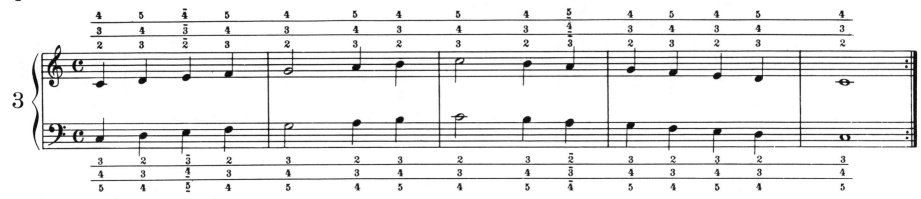

Substitution

The substitution must be made immediately upon arriving at the new note.

Transpose into all keys.

Transpose into all keys.

M. & R. Co. 5091

Glissando

Finger glissando, from black to white key.

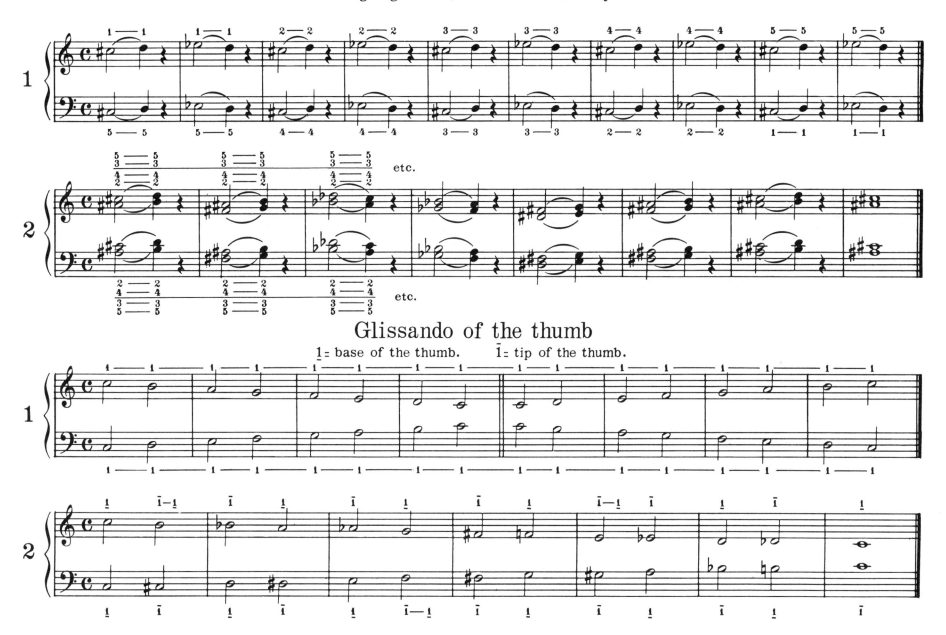

Glissando of the thumb

1̲ = base of the thumb.   1̄ = tip of the thumb.

Rules for performance

1) A repeated note loses one half of its value in a quick or moderate tempo.

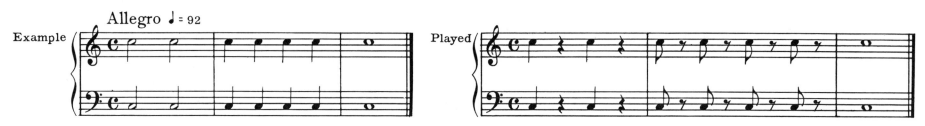

Fugue in E.   J. S. Bach (Peters III)

2) In a slow tempo a repeated note loses a quarter of its value.

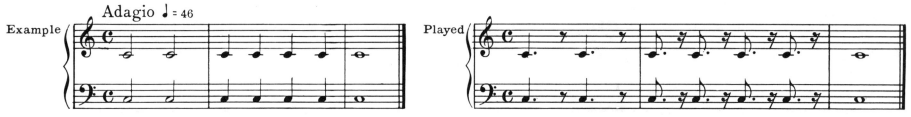

Choralprel: Christus der uns selig macht.   J. S. Bach (Peters V)

M. & R. Co. 5091

3) A repeated note loses the value of the dot.

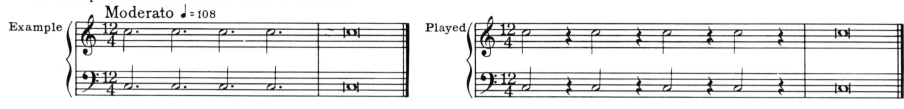

Canzona. J. S. Bach (Peters IV)

4) When two adjacent parts have a note in common, the latter of the two is treated as a tied note.

Choral in A. C. Franck.

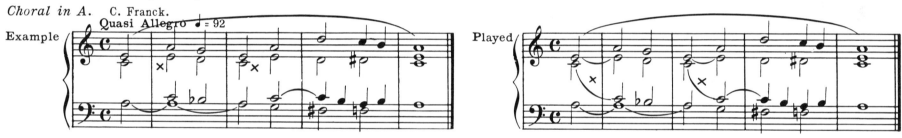

5) In "Pleno" or in comparatively loud, strongly rhythmical passages, successive chords are played detached.

Toccata in F. J. S. Bach (Peters III)

6) Skips of octaves, particularly downward skips are played detached at the end of phrases, when the first note occurs on the strong beat, and the second is followed by a rest.

Choralprel: Herr Christ, der einige Gottes sohn. J. S. Bach (Peters V)

Regarding more extended rules of performance and ornamentation see "Ars Organi" complete organ method in three parts. C. F. Peters Corp., N.Y.

M. & R. Co. 5091

III. TWO-PART MANUAL PLAYING

Now, My Tongue, the Myst'ry Telling *

Flor Peeters

Moderato ♩ = 92

1 I Diapason 8'

*This melody is also known as a setting of *Tantum ergo Sacramentum*.

M. & R. Co. 5091

God My Father, Loving Me

Flor Peeters

Father, We Thank Thee for the Night

Flor Peeters

O *Sacred Head*

Flor Peeters

O Sacred Head

J. Pachelbel **1653-1706**

Invention

Allegro moderato ♩ = 80

Flor Peeters

6 I Foundations
8′ 4′ 2′
Mixt.

Choralprel: *Warum sollt ich mich denn grämen*

played:

J. G. Walther **1684-1748**

* The trill is represented by the following signs: 〰, 〰, 〰, or *tr*, *beginning always with the upper note in classical organ literature*, up to the time of the Manheimer School.   See study of ornamentation in "Ars Organi" complete organ method in **3** parts – C.F. Peters Corporation, New York.

14

Versus VI Toni

A. V. den Kerckhoven 1627-1673

8

II { Princ. 8′ 4′ 2′
     { Mixt.

Invention

Flor Peeters

Partita: *O Gott, du frommer Gott*

J. S. Bach **1685-1750**

(1) played: (2) played: or

IV. ELEMENTARY PEDAL EXERCISES

To indicate pedalling the following signs are used: ⋀ for the toe, ⋃ for the heel. When printed above the note, the sign indicates the use of the right foot; below the notes, the left foot. *Attack*: by touching, attack and release the notes quickly and decisively. Keep the feet in contact with the keys. Never move the legs but only the feet so that the ankle acts as a fulcrum. For the following exercises keep knees and heels together.

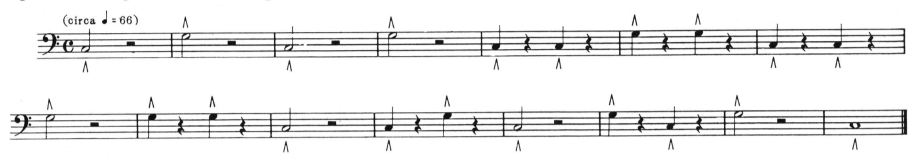

Exercises for alternate toes.

Exercises with different intervals (long pedals)

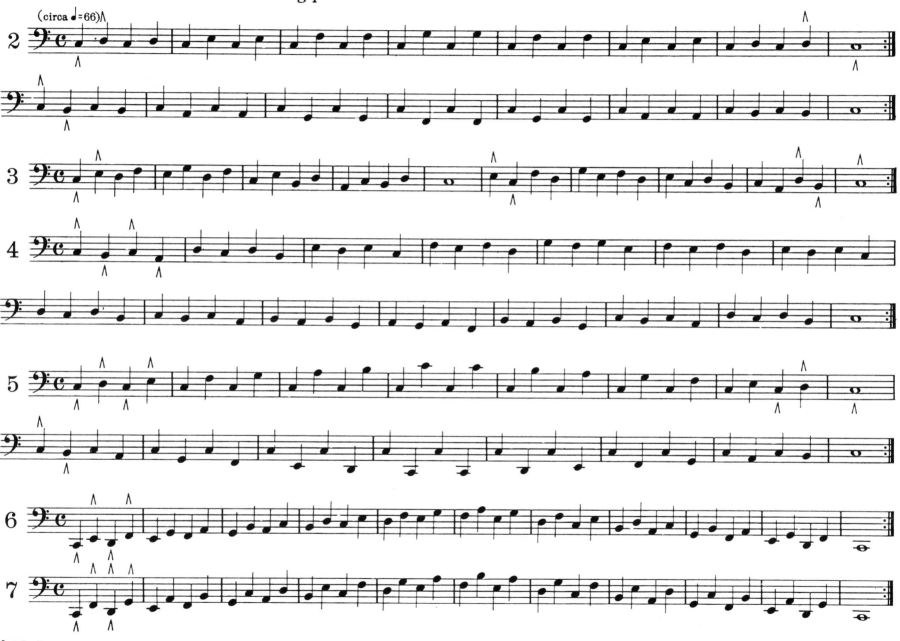

M. & R. Co. 5091

20

Repeated notes.

Exercises with different intervals (long and short pedals)*

* The "long" pedals are the equivalent of the white notes on the manual keyboard and the "short" pedals are the same as the black notes on the manual keyboard.

M. & R. Co. 5091

Four Pedal Studies (Toes Only)

Flor Peeters

24

M. & R. Co. 5091

V. THREE-PART PLAYING

Preparatory two-part exercises for each hand separately.   The fingering above the notes applies to the right hand, below the notes, to the left hand.

M. & R. Co. 5091

THREE-PART MANUAL PLAYING

Prelude

Flor Peeters

Choralprel: Now, My Tongue *

Moderato ♩ = 66

Flor Peeters

I
Gemshorn 8'
Flute oct. 4'

2

* See note on page 8.

30

Choralprel: *Allein Gott in der Höh sei Ehr*

F. W. Zachow 1663-1712

Verset, Magnificat IV-Toni

G. Carissimi 1605-1674

Choralprel: Wie schön leuchtet der Morgenstern

D. Buxtehude 1637-1707

5 III { Bourdon 8'
Quintad. 4'
Flute 1' }

Choralprel: *O Sacred Head*

J. Pachelbel **1653-1706**

Choralprel: O Sacred Head

Flor Peeters

Invention on "Veni Creator"

Flor Peeters

40

Fughetta on: Gottes Sohn ist kommen

J. S. Bach 1685-1750

9

Bourdon 8'
Flute 4'
Octave 2'
Cymbel

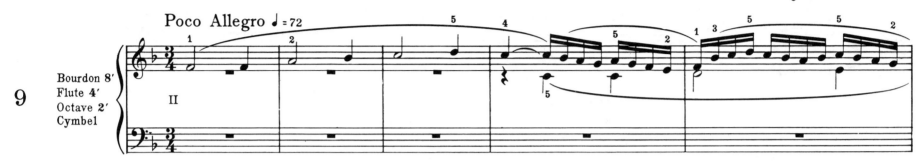

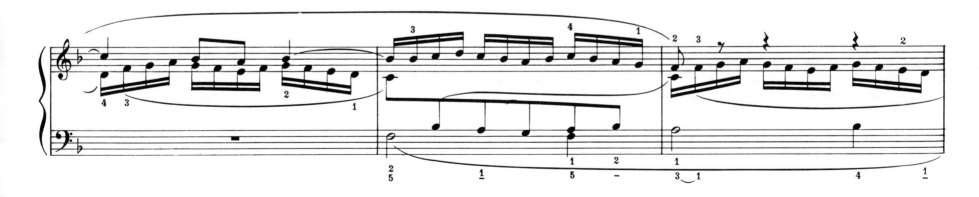

M. & R. Co. 5091

Choralprel: O Come, All Ye Faithful

Flor Peeters

Attack

44

a) Crossings

The signs Λ̄ and Ū̄ indicate the crossing of the feet in front.
The signs Λ̲ and Ṵ indicate the crossing from behind.

b) Substitutions. 1) of the feet. 2) of toe and heel.

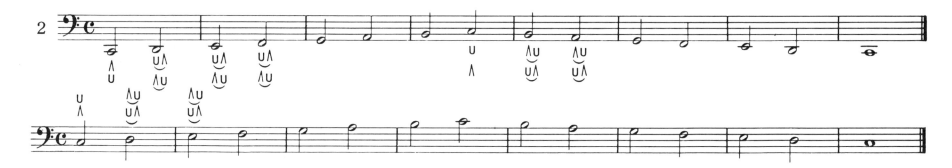

c) Glissandos. (between short and long pedals)

M. & R. Co. 5091

Four pedal studies for toe and heel

Flor Peeters

48

O Come, All Ye Faithful

Flor Peeters

M. & R. Co. 5091

VII. TWO-PART MANUAL AND PEDAL PLAYING

God, My Father

Flor Peeters

4

Father, We Thank Thee

Flor Peeters

5

O Sacred Head

Flor Peeters

6

II Flute 8' 4'
Octave 2'
R. H.

Ped.
Bassoon 16'
Flute 4'

Interlude

Moderato ♩ = 84

J. Habert 1833-1896

7

I Foundations 8' 4'
L. H.

Ped.
16' 8'

Prelude

J. Habert **1833-1896**

8

M. & R. Co. 5091

VIII. THREE-PART MANUAL AND PEDAL PLAYING

Jesus Christ Is Risen Today

Flor Peeters

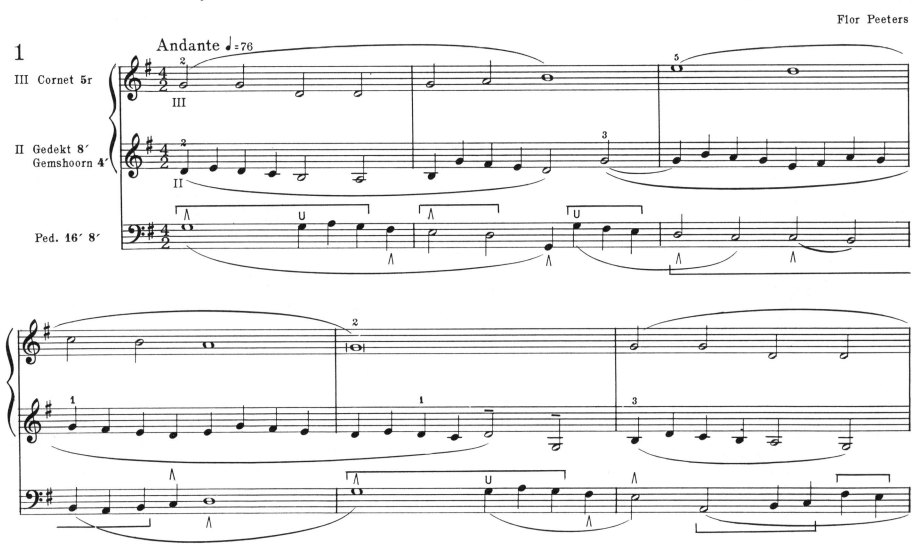

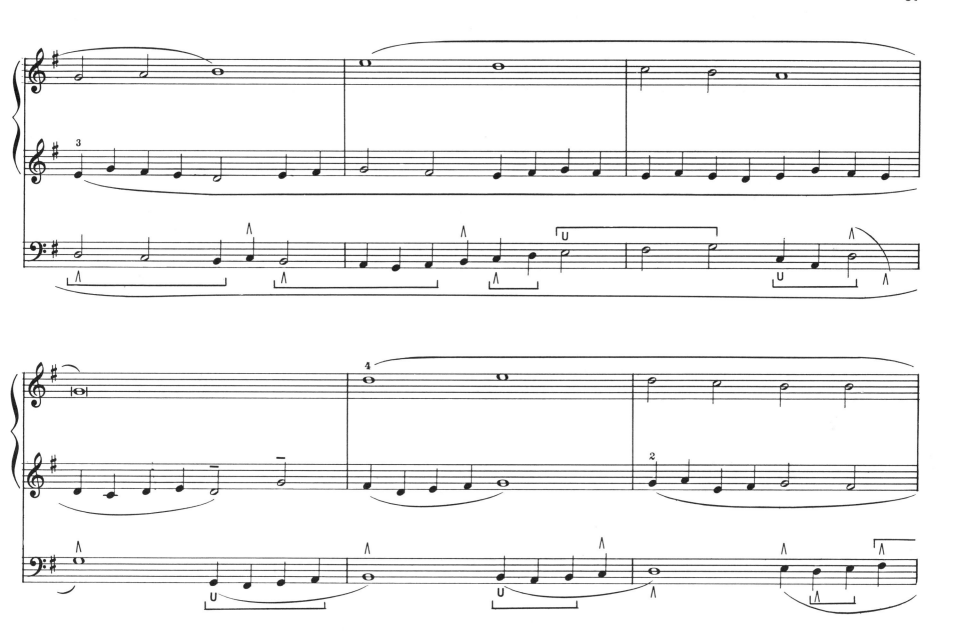

Creator alme siderum

J. Titelouse **1563-1633**

2

II Trumpet 8′

III Princip. 8′ 4′

Brd. 16′ 8′

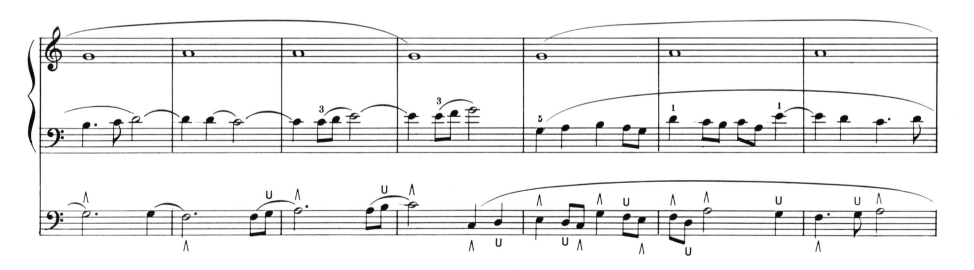

60

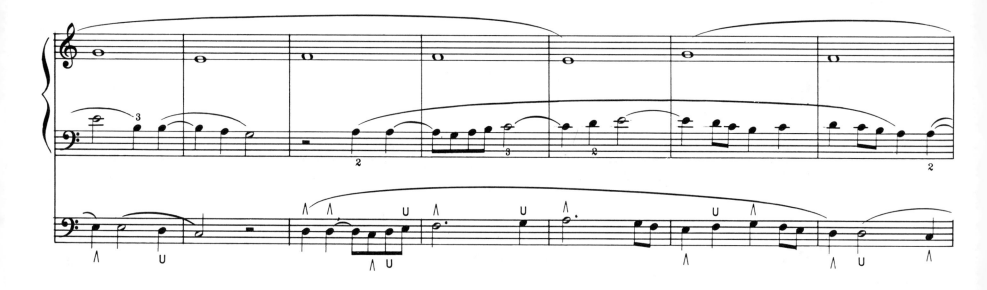

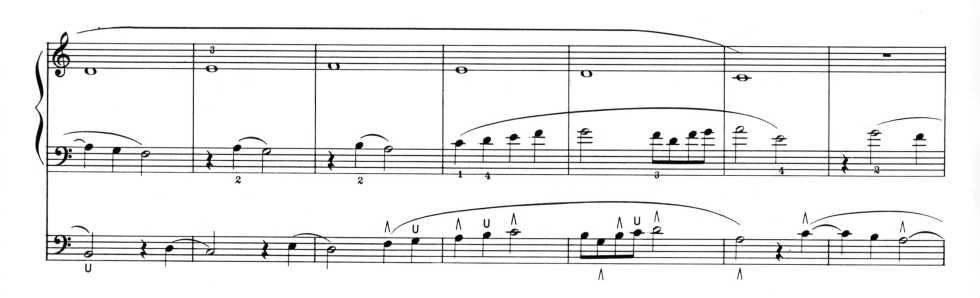

O Sacred Head

Flor Peeters

3

Andante ♩=63

III Oboe 8'

Salic. 8'
Rohrflöte 4'

Soft 16' 8'

63

M.&R.Co.5091

Jesus Christ Is Risen Today

Flor Peeters

65

M.&R.Co.5091

God Father, Praise and Glory

Flor Peeters

68

M.&R.Co.5091

Choralprel: Vom Himmel hoch

6

Allegro moderato ♩ = 80

F.W. Zachow 1663-1712

II
Bourdon 8′
Flute 4′ 2′

Bourdon 16′
Vox humana 8′
Flute 2′

Jesus Christ Is Risen Today

Flor Peeters

J. L. Krebs 1804-1880

Andante

Choralprel: Vom Himmel hoch

J. Pachelbel 1653-1706

Choralprel: Unto Thee I Cry, O Lord Jesus

J. S. Bach 1685-1750

IX. FOUR-PART MANUAL PLAYING

Holy God, We Praise Thy Name!

Flor Peeters

Versus IV-Toni

A. de Cabezon **1510-1566**

84

Versus I Toni

J.K.Kerll 1627-1693

M. &R. Co. 5091

Choralprel: *Liebster Jesu, Wir sind hier*

J. S. Bach 1685-1750

Versus V Toni

J. Pachelbel 1653-1706

X. FOUR-PART MANUAL AND PEDAL PLAYING

Choralprel: Now, My Tongue *

Flor Peeters

1

III Oboe 8' Solo

II Salic. 8'
Soft Flute 4

Ped. 16' 8'

* See note on page **29**.

M. & R. Co. **5091**

Dernier Kyrie *

F. Couperin 1632-1701

2

Andante ♩ = 54

I Foundations 8′ 4′ 2′
Mixtures

Foundations
Ped.   16′ 8′ 4′
Mixt.,Reeds 8′ 4′

* Based on last Kyrie of Mass. No. IV of the Gregorian Kyriale.

M. & R. Co. 5091

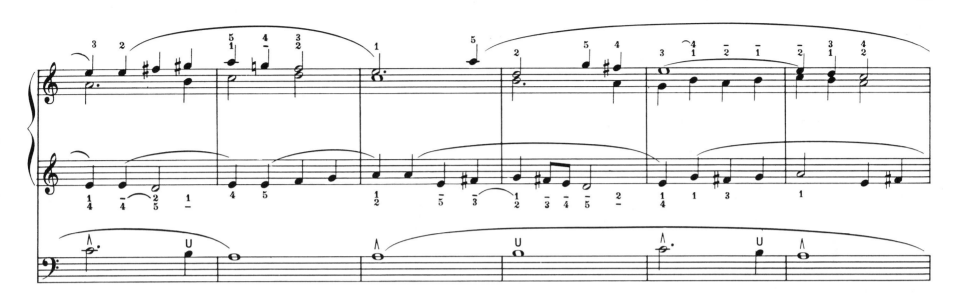

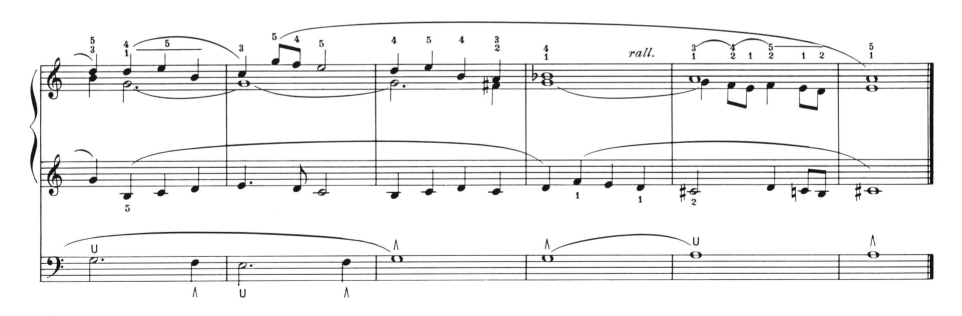

M. & R. Co. 5091

Herr Gott, lass dich erbarmen

H. Isaac (1450-1517)

M. & R. Co. 5091

Choralprel: *Jesu meine Freude*

J. S. Bach (1685-1750)

Choralprel: *Gelobet seist du, Jesu Christ*

J. S. Bach **1685-1750**

5

III Trumpet 8'

1 Gemshorn 8'
  Octave 4'

Ped. 16' 8'

M. & R. Co. 5091

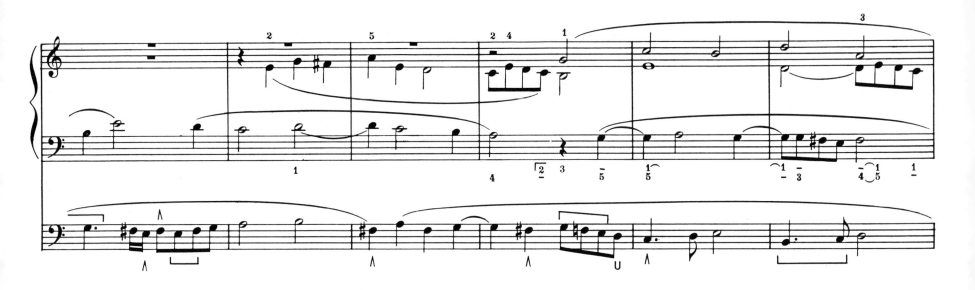

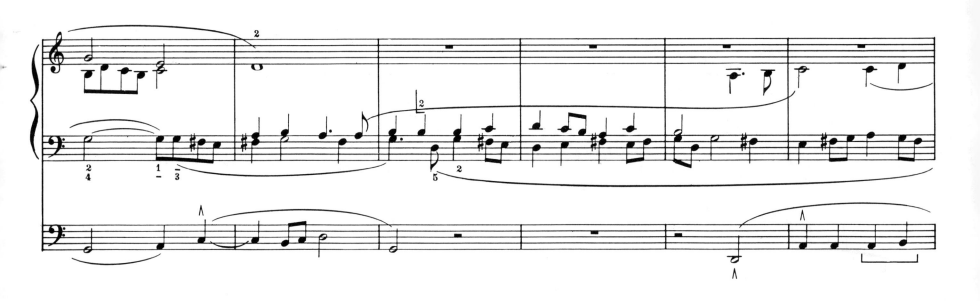

M. & R. Co. 5091

Prelude and Fugue in C

J. S. Bach 1685-1750

Prelude
Allegro vivo ♩ = 80

6

I (& II, III)
Foundations 8' 4'
Mixt., Cymb.
Soft reeds 8' 4'

Ped. 16' 8' 4'
& I, II, III

M. & R. Co. 5091